LT

D1487194

FORCES ON LEADERSHIP

by
Michael C. Giammatteo
and
Dolores M. Giammatteo

National Association of Secondary School Principals
Reston, Va.

a -   other same
189
PB159 208

ABOUT THE AUTHORS: Michael C. Giammatteo and Dolores M. Giammatteo have held a variety of administrative positions in education, including state and national levels. Dolores is the director of the women's programs and Michael is the executive director of the Sylvan Institute of Mental Health and Family Services, Vancouver, Wash.

Contents

Foreword

SCHOOL ADMINISTRATORS by virtue of the fact that they are responsible for educational institutions—their operation and their destiny—are automatically leaders. "But how good a leader am I?" is a question they often express in their search for ways to improve themselves and their effectiveness.

Answering that question is not simple. Defining leadership and listing its characteristics can be difficult. What applies to one leader may not apply to another. What makes an outstanding symphony director or a successful coach is not necessarily what makes an effective president, governor, or mayor. History is replete with examples of people who succeeded as leaders in one activity and then failed as they moved into other areas of endeavor.

We think this monograph by Michael and Dolores Giammatteo pursues the subject of leadership in a way that readers will find not only interesting but also helpful in their understanding of the concepts behind leadership. The authors, whose *Executive Well-Being: Stress and Administrators* (NASSP, 1980) was received so well by educators, take a close look at what makes an educational leader—the forces that come to play daily from within, from those being led, and from the environment.

Especially different in this monograph are the self-guided exercises. Readers are not left to hypothesize the principles and to conjecture how they fit or do not fit certain profiles. By using the 15 exercises, readers will learn much about themselves and their effectiveness as school leaders.

As the Giammatteos advise in their preface, use the material in this monograph as a tool, then probe, analyze, and reflect. We think it will be a valuable part of your professional reading.

Thomas F. Koerner
Editor and Director of Publications
NASSP

Preface

THE SCHOOL DISTRICTS are as responsible for their principals' successes or failures as are the principals themselves. We in leadership roles often ignore this simple concept, "Leadership performance depends on the organizational situation and current cultural norms as well as on the leader."

Throughout history good educational leadership has been the focus of intense interest, controversy, and speculation. The successes and failures of schools, districts, and even broader societies have been attributed to the skills, behaviors, characteristics, and values of the teachers and educational leaders. Only recently have evaluations, school surveys, research, and development focused on this interest in an attempt to better understand the nature of educational leadership. The general outcome of these focused efforts is the conclusion that educational leadership is a very complex cluster of behaviors and there indeed is no single method for effective leadership.

Why then, another leadership book when we cannot be prescriptive?

We believe that leaders do not just materialize; rather they are educated and trained in process skills and to see cause and effect, as well as to grow and develop personally.

In this monograph we focus on the forces within a leader, within those being led, and within the environments affecting the principal. We are not talking about elected leaders or about those who rise naturally in social or disaster situations, but about educational leaders who work in organizational settings.

The principal is assumed to be an expert in education. However, a portion of this book requests involvement in brief but insightful self-guided experiential learning. In this type of learning, knowledge can be acquired which is not easily conveyed to others, but which does influence our knowledge base.

Please use this text as a tool. Tools demand handling, use, and experimentation, for self-mastery. We encourage probing, exploring, analyzing, and reflecting.

Michael C. Giammatteo
Dolores M. Giammatteo

1. Introduction: Forces On Leaders

EDUCATIONAL LEADERS, like leaders generally, have certain skills and techniques which work especially well for them. Often they try to pass these skills along to others in their institutions. Many also try to instill the same qualities and attitudes in the people who work with them. But, good leaders have to allow for a number of individual differences, such as training and intellectual differences. What works for one person may not be the best method for another.

Whether we are aware of it or not, most of our administrative style in working through and with staff, other adults, and students is affected by several forces. In this monograph we will discuss many important factors: early childhood influences; past experience; leadership training; the present administrative and work environment; and the cultural environment.

We will also briefly discuss important forces, with self-assessment devices and discussion techniques to aid in identifying change strategies administrators may wish to consider. The forces are summarized in three broad categories:

I. *Forces Within the Leader*

There will be a description of leadership and an exploration of the forces within a person that affect adult leadership behaviors.

Personal assessment profiles will help determine what causes us to lead as we do in our role.

II. *Forces Within Those Being Led*

Changing roles of parents, students, family, community, and teacher groups will be explored in terms of their views and our tasks of educational leadership.

Forces related to work ethics and followership that often appear as resistance to educational leadership will be explored with an eye to practical responses administrators can use to reduce these forces.

III. *Forces Within the Environment*

A review of the predicted needs for people of the next decade along with a review of the world outside of the protected school will provide a practical guide to administrators who frequently interact with curriculum advisers and who often are called to discuss such factors in public meetings. This section of the monograph also points to challenges and trends that the practical leader will want to clearly understand.

The definition we have of any role causes us to react and act. A brief concept outline of what modern management people consider leadership, and personal profiles and questions for examining the forces that are operative in most decisions are included in this first section.

Some Concepts of Leadership

MODERN DEFINITION OF LEADERSHIP:

In basic terms, leadership is the activity of helping others work toward common goals or purposes. Today, the experts in leadership are the ones who best know how to release the creative talents of those with whom they work. In earlier years, the expert in leadership was considered to be the one who best knew the answers. Now, terminology has changed from "directing and controlling" to "involving and motivating."

Leadership may be regarded as a series of functions that: (1) builds and maintains the group, (2) gets the job done, (3) helps the group feel comfortable and at ease (looking after physical setting, acquaintanceship, etc.), (4) helps to set and clearly define objectives, and (5) cooperatively works toward these objectives.

LEADERSHIP MYTHS:

In earlier years it was assumed that leaders possessed certain special traits or characteristics. Many studies were made in an effort to correlate the leadership capacity or potential of an individual with these personal attributes. While some definable personal characteristics have been linked to leaders in certain situations, these studies haven't been successful in providing a formula for leadership selection. The modern concept is that leadership is functional or "job centered." We should ask then, "What does an effective leader do?" rather than, "What kind of person will be a good leader?"

We have often heard the statement, "That person is a natural-born leader." We know now that a leader in one situation may have very little leadership ability in another. A guide on a mountain climbing expedition might not be a very effective school board chairman.

THE ART AND SCIENCE OF LEADERSHIP:

The ability to work effectively with groups in a leadership role can be learned through conscientious effort, study, and practice. Leadership is both an art and a science. The scientific principles are learnable. Therefore, any of us may do a better job of leadership if we understand and conscientiously practice some of these principles.

The art of leadership is the way in which we apply leadership principles. We know that there is variation in the manner in which we carry on any activity. This is apparent in such everyday activities as playing a musical instrument, going to school, cooking a meal, or even fishing. In each of these activities, as in leadership, learning and practicing certain principles will help, but people vary in the degree to which they approach application. Students of human relationships have identified many functions or skills that are based on sound leadership principles.

SKILLS OF LEADERSHIP:

The following are some of the skills that are important to learn and to practice.

1. *Skills of personal behavior.* The effective leader:
   - Is sensitive to feelings of the group.
   - Identifies self with the needs of the group.
   - Learns to listen attentively.

- Refrains from criticizing or ridiculing members' suggestions.
- Helps each member feel important and needed.
- Should not argue.

2. *Skills of communication.* The effective leader:
   - Makes sure that everyone understands not only what is needed but why.
   - Makes good communication with the group a routine part of the job.

3. *Skills in equality.* The effective leader recognizes that:
   - Everyone is important.
   - Leadership is to be shared and is not a monopoly.
   - A leader grows when leadership functions are dispersed.

4. *Skills of organization.* The effective leader helps the group:
   - Develop long-range and short-range objectives.
   - Break big problems into small ones.
   - Share opportunities and responsibilities.
   - Plan, act, follow up and evaluate.

5. *Skills of Self Examination.* The effective leader:
   - Is aware of motivations and motives guiding actions.
   - Is aware of members' levels of hostility and tolerance so that appropriate counter measures are taken.
   - Is aware of their fact-finding behavior.
   - Helps the group to be aware of their own forces, attitudes and values.

These leadership concepts also apply to non-educational and private sector leaders. Institutions such as schools must clearly understand leaders as well as the concept of leadership. Challenges to meet new student needs, methods, and forms of organization with other demands require flexible and innovative responses.

The ever-growing awareness that definitions often cause expectancies that may lead to role conflict is also a challenge. For example, if in your mind you are a teacher and your role changes to that of an administrator, you may still be operating as a teacher. The principal's role is obviously important, yet the success of the principal's performance is often not evident. Even less evident is the concern for this educational leader's personal unique history. Indeed, many social observers feel that organi-

4

zations often have serious negative impacts on the mental hea of the people who work with them.

One negative force, which requests we "fit in and not rock the boat," can often inhibit change. Change is what educational leadership is all about: The ability to be secure enough to allow progress. Good leaders must keep their eyes on results, not just methods. If a new leader occasionally does something different, keep in mind it's the only possible way to improve. It also is the only possible way to keep capable and creative people happy and working *with* the organization, not against it. This leadership force is known simply as "Open Mindedness."

Sometimes the emotional and organizational costs are too much when a change is suggested and the potential gains are too small. This is when the leader uses judgment. The leadership force of "Maintenance," keeping the status quo, can also be a convenient excuse to be negative. The more new ideas you and your people can try, the more good ones you will discover.

The force of an open-minded administrator stimulates others. The norm of having safe and low profile administrators who have little faith in ideas or others often results in a district having administrators who lack faith in themselves.

As educational administrators we must also be aware that other people's jobs usually look easier to us than our own, just as our jobs look easy to others. To add irony to this negative force that perceives our role as simplistic, the more talented we as administrators are, the easier our jobs look.

In Chapter Two we will present some assessment techniques that will explore the forces that make leaders what they are or are trying to be in the educational setting.

Knowledge of the "self" and understanding of the power and effects of one's behavior on others is a demand of the educational leader in today's world. We no longer can be benevolent dictators but must be negotiation and representative-oriented. The greater the difference between forces within principals and their perception of what the external school environment demands, the less the potential for effective joint social action or effective leadership.

2. Forces Within Leaders

A CENTRAL VALUE of our society is that people should engage in meaningful work. Many rewards that society provides such as recognition, status, prestige, and respect are intimately tied to the kind of work people do.

Work titles determine how people are identified by others and thus how they identify themselves. It is difficult for people to develop a positive sense of self worth, a positive image or a sense of dignity, if what they do goes against their own values or is not positively valued by their organization or society. It is even more harmful if the inner self, the organization, or the society devalues the work of the leader.

The need is for administrative people, especially at building levels, to realize they do not work *on* a situation; rather they work *inside* the situation and indeed may be central characters. Principals who don't realize the fact that they not only influence, but are influenced by situations, become blind and isolated in a social sense. The buildings may operate "around" them.

Therefore, one of our aims is to provide awareness of why and how people influence and are influenced.

Where do you place control?

Many teachers' tasks may be *internally* initiated, and because of lack of other adult feedback, their worth would have to meet

6

with their own internal values. However, when teachers become administrators, their worth may be judged more by *external* forces, such as compliance with district regulations and federal guidelines.

This first profile is designed to assess the locus of control of your current behavior. Is it primarily internal or external?

While outer-directed leaders are capable of success, they are quickly put out of effective action by the least bit of criticism. When making a decision, they also would give in to the option least likely to create the implications of failure. Since they are susceptible to spending more time protecting themselves than working on solutions, they often increase their own possibilities for inadequacy. They may even become more outer-directed, delegating for the wrong reasons.

Inner-directed people sense that they largely determine what happens to them. They feel a sense of control over their inner resources, actions, attitudes, and thoughts after actions are taken. They are more adaptable and reality oriented than outer-directed leaders. However, when under severe stress they will tend to become disturbed and blame themselves for what occurs. Consequently, they interpret events as stressful more often than do outer-directed people.

Public administrators who are inner-directed carry around a great deal of shame and guilt. They become non-functional in their roles and often are preoccupied with the "rightness" of a choice or action. Many times they get lost in nickel and dime details and fail to see the overview or bigger picture. They have a strong tendency to become excessively introspective. They look for causes, reasons, and over-analyze insignificant and minor factors.

As a leader, it is essential to know which buttons your subordinates, ordinates, and superiors can push. Often the inner-directiveness that made you excel in one role may have to be used differently in your school principal or leadership role.

To know the locus of control that guides you is vital. To know when to be inner or outer directed is the judgmental factor only you can develop by administrative experience. Your reactions to assessment as well as the style in which you carry out your response all become part of leadership.

Locus of Control Profile: Exercise #1

This form is designed to assess the personality forces within you that direct or stimulate your actions. These internal forces that you bring to your leadership position help or hinder your functioning at work. First, go through each statement and rate yourself as to the manner in which you typically react or feel in each of the situations. (Place 1, 2, 3, 4, or 5 in the blank before each item, please.)

1 = Never	2 = Infrequently	3 = Sometimes	4 = Frequently	5 = Always
(10% or less would not react this way)	(70% no) I would not react or feel that way.	(50% either way)	(70% yes) I would react or feel that way.	(10% or less would react this way)

1. ____ There really is little I can do to influence the decisions of those in authority.
2. ____ My work is less productive when I have to interact with others.
3. ____ What happens in my life is because of circumstance and fate.
4. ____ If given a chance I like to work with others.
5. ____ Luck has a lot to do with success.
6. ____ Since it is impossible to try to change a large organization, I tend to go along with current procedures.
7. ____ I can't do the things I want to in life because of my work.
8. ____ I do like to interact with others to reach decisions that affect my work.

Interpretations:

Add up the ratings of questions 1, 2, 3, 6, 7.

If you marked in a rating of 4 or 5 for each of the five items noted for a score of 20 to 25, you are probably outer-directed.

A score of 5 to 10 implies you are inner-directed.

The higher the number, the more you respond to external pressures and control, and the more you feel out of control. The lower scores 5, 6, 7 are indicative of people very self-oriented in terms of decisions and where they feel control is located.

How do you assess truth?

The following profile is designed to aid you in reviewing several potential ways you might assess "facts" in a given situation. Please keep in mind your Locus of Control Profile results. Public administration requires a tolerance of external control forces. Also, note that the five generally used fact finding techniques are external in origin.

Fact Finding Styles: Exercise #2

You should never assume that the best or the only solution to a problem will be found solely within the membership. Despite the vast resources of your members, look beyond your organization for help when it is clear that extending your search for facts will improve your understanding of the situation. Become aware of all environmental sources of information.

There are numerous ways to "Fact Find" or gather information. Here are some standard sources and methods of procuring reliable facts and information.

A B C   1.   *AUTHORITIES:* (Experts) Two or three are better than one. Select them from different philosophies or allegiances. (A wise man once said, "When you have a committee of 10 who all think alike, get rid of nine of them.")

A B C   2.   *DOCUMENTS:* Bylaws, codes, policies, minutes, agreements, contracts, earlier studies, methods or ideas. Are there any clues from current policy, or have other groups with a similar problem employed an idea which could fit your organization's needs?

A B C   2.   *PUBLICATIONS:* Reference books. Avoid accepting a single authority or author.

A B C   4.   *GENERAL ELECTION/VOTE:* A traditional way of obtaining popular opinion. Validity is limited to the opinion, judgment or will of those voting, but it is nevertheless an indicator.

A B C   5.   *SURVEYS/QUESTIONNAIRES:* Design them to be brief, clear and easy to score. Consider scoring by mark-sense equipment, IBM cards, or boxes along the margin. Get design help from experts. Run a pilot tryout on at least 10 people before deciding on a final format.

Now, consider these situations:

    A. You are asked to fire a poor worker who happens to be a minority member.

    B. You are asked to make a decision about a new piece of equipment.

    C. You want to make a personal decision.

Situation A demands acceptance and tolerance of external control in terms of legal demands and pressure groups and single issue groups.

Situation B also demands a tolerance of external control. For example, safety factors may be mandated about the piece of equipment that would limit its use to only highly qualified persons.

Situation C is where one has the option of being guided by external or internal forces.

Which fact finding style would you use to make these decisions? Circle the letter next to the style, indicating which situation(s) would best be handled by that particular style.

One form of truth finding or fact determination comes from within your own experience base or from your own intuition. All the others on the fact finding assessment sheet are based on administrative behavior that calls for external support for type A and B situations. Know which forces are at work within you. You are in a leadership position. Your view of a leader may not be the same as your followers'.

How tolerant are you?

Often we may be internally motivated and so much noticed in our roles that we are promoted into an administrative role which demands a great deal of tolerance of external locus of control type of behavior.

Tolerance Assessment: Exercise #3

Items	Dislike	Can Tolerate
1. People who want to change just for the sake of change.		
2. People who believe there is only one right way.		
3. People who do not appreciate what this job has done for them.		
4. People who overstep their job descriptions or roles.		
5. People who are always expressing views contrary to mine.		
6. People who complain all the time but do nothing to make a situation better.		
7. People who value success above all other values.		
8. People who are unwilling to listen to rational ideas and data.		

Check one response.

Scoring information for the Tolerance Assessment form is illustrative of the responses people in management, supervision and other leadership roles have granted us in workshop and university classes. You are your own expert so please keep that in mind as you interpret your responses.

Add up all of the responses marked *Dislike*. Multiply that score by 5 to obtain a total form score. If you marked 2 items *Dislike* then you would multiply 2 × 5 for score of 10 points. You would then read the interpretation paragraph under *10 points or Less* for hints about forces operative within you, the leader.

Assess yourself and talk it over with a friend. Feedback allows for feed forward.

10 points or less

You generally have an open mind toward most controversial issues and maintain a live-and-let-live attitude toward people and their values. Your easy-going and accepting attitudes are sometimes seen as indifference or a refusal on your part to take a stand on issues. You tend to be informed and knowledgeable in many areas and will often suspend judgment about right or wrong and good or bad because you feel that you have little basis for making a sound decision. People will tend to express their opinions to you, or turn to you for advice, because they feel that you will listen with a sympathetic ear and will not judge them harshly.

11 to 22 points

Like most people you tend to be less flexible and more subjective in important areas that have deep personal meaning for you. Although you are willing to accept change even when doing so means giving up long-standing beliefs, your ability to make the transition takes time. You usually are able to recognize when you hold intolerant views, but you find it emotionally difficult to give up these views completely. It is likely that in those areas where you are most threatened by change you will look for proof that your opinions and attitudes are correct.

23 points or more

You tend to be quite conservative in your approach to new ideas and prefer to stick to conventional ideas and values. You maintain high standards and will often disapprove of those who do not meet these standards. You may find it difficult to see or accept opposing viewpoints, especially in areas dealing with social conduct. Since you are uncomfortable with change, you tend to be suspicious of those who are in favor of altering the traditional ways of doing things. Although it is not necessary to agree with the opinions of others, by keeping an open mind you can gain the satisfaction of knowing that you weighed both sides of a question before coming to a decision.

How hostile are you?

If we "act" tolerant but actually are not, we must be aware of our internal force of hostility. Hostility and resentment build up when we have a negative feeling, but we cannot express that feeling because of role or situation. For example, if you feel frustrated 90 percent of the time at work but have to act tolerant and let the external forces control your actions, you may be stocking up resentment. If you can voice that frustration to a trusted friend 80 percent of the time, you will have minimal hostility or resentment. Held-in hurts cause us to be hostile.

Hostility Assessment: Exercise #4

Items	Check one response	
	Frequently	Rarely
1. When I don't want to do a task, I tend to forget to do it.		
2. I tend to confront subjects or concepts that are embarrassing to others.		
3. I tend to do things that bother others.		
4. I seem to make people feel guilty or ill at ease by what I say.		
5. I ask questions of others often knowing they can not give a response or do not know the answer.		
6. I tend to say things in a manner that hurts the feelings of others.		
7. I tend to do things to show people up in social, recreational, as well as in work situations.		
8. I get upset when others foul up my pre-determined plans.		

Scoring information for the Hostility Assessment form again is illustrative, can vary from day to day, and is useful for leaders who hope to understand their roles in the process of administration.

Score your response according to the chart to obtain a total score which you can interpret via the following three paragraphs.

Item No.	Weighted Score	
	Frequently	Rarely
1.	8	1
2.	10	1
3.	10	1
4.	10	1
5.	10	1
6.	8	1
7.	10	1
8.	8	1

(Sub Total) ____ + ____(Sub Total) =

Total Form Score _____

50 points or more

The saving grace about your hostilities is that you can admit them and that they are often out in the open so others have a clear idea about you. Those who allow for your resentments and fault finding do so more out of loyalty, or a desire to rehabilitate you, rather than because of your pleasant disposition. Some people may find you convenient because you are able to express the same hostilities that they often feel, but are too timid to express. You will often find that your grievances are a greater source of pain to yourself than to others.

20 to 49 points

The situations that frustrate you and produce anger are more or less common to most people. You generally manage to conceal your hostility or dampen its effect on others. You are usually not quarrelsome and irritable and you can be fairly reasonable when others frustrate or offend you; nevertheless, you are not likely to turn the other cheek when you feel that someone has taken unfair advantage of you. You tend to consider the feelings of others and in most instances will not deliberately act to upset others.

19 points or less

Your good natured, forgiving temperament can frustrate as well as please others. People are usually attracted to your patience and understanding, especially when these qualities are directed to them. When you do not become indignant or express anger in situations which tend to upset others, you may be mistakenly described as timid or meek. You must be careful not to suppress feelings of resentment, especially to those you feel dependent upon, for these angry feelings may come out at inappropriate moments, much to everyone's surprise.

How motivated are you?

Our motivational forces differ from year to year and from role to role. However, it is good to know which internal motivators are at work in us as we try to administer in a pluralistic culture and to various in-school groups. We will analyze three motivation traits: power, achievement, and belonging.

Motivational Analysis: Exercise #5

Please indicate how thoroughly each item describes both your present job, and your "ideal" job. In the space provided, write the number *from zero to five* which is most appropriate, using the following scale:

5—*Extremely true* of my present (or ideal) job
4—*Very true* of my present (or ideal) job
3—*Somewhat true* of my present (or ideal) job
2—*Not very true* of my present (or ideal) job
1—*Only slightly true* of my present (or ideal) job
0—Not true at all

TRAIT A—ACHIEVEMENT

	Present Job	Ideal Job
1. I get frequent feedback on the measureable results I am producing.		
2. I can constantly improve on the quality of work I produce by finding better ways to do things.		
3. If I don't do a job or task as well as I would like, I get a chance to try it again and improve.		
4. For the most part, I work alone.		

	Present Job	Ideal Job
5. My boss allows me to set the standards for much of my own performance.		
6. There is very little which is repetitive or routine in my work.		
7. Personal productivity counts more than personality.		
8. I have extensive control over the factors which affect the results of my work.		
TOTAL		

35 points or more

You tend to think in terms of results and may not want to spend time planning. You set high standards and thus may wish to do many tasks yourself. You may be practical and right to the point, but unwittingly be insensitive to others. You are uncomfortable with instability and want to work productively and get the job done.

29 to 34 points

You generally feel a short-term viewpoint is practical and that task completion is vital, but is not the total leadership game. You are open to feedback and tend to be good at calculating how much give and take a situation will tolerate.

28 or fewer points

You may need to focus on tasks you feel should be done. You also have great difficulty accepting instability but do little to change the situation. This type of profile is good for the person serving only as a representative.

TRAIT B—BELONGING

	Present Job	Ideal Job
1. There is a strong sense of friendliness and fellowship in the group I work with, with considerable sharing of enjoyable experiences.		

	Present Job	Ideal Job
2. Being able to understand and help with other's personal problems is very important to my success.		
3. There is a lot of interaction with others in my job.		
4. It is important that I keep friendly relations with others.		
5. I am expected to smooth over conflicts which arise in my work situation.		
6. I am not expected to produce more than the other people who work with me.		
7. I have ample opportunity to socialize and pass the time with the people I work with.		
8. I must have the cooperation of others to get my work done.		
TOTAL		

34 points or more

You like to involve others even at the risk of reducing the chance for task completion. You tend to be supportive, but may develop emotional territory and find it hard to let go. You work well and the need to belong is a constant motivator. Your need to belong may at times reduce objectivity.

29 to 33 points

You tend to want to belong but often do things that are based more on the fear of hurting people than on the concept of task completion. You also can separate yourself from a situation better than the person who scores high in this motivator.

28 or fewer points

Others may feel you are cold and isolated or hard to get to know. You may not need close friendships at work.

TRAIT C—POWER

	Present Job	Ideal Job
1. I have considerable authority over others.		
2. My part of the organization is very well organized with clear channels of communication.		
3. I make decisions which others are expected to follow.		
4. Good performance is rewarded by promotion to a position with increased authority.		
5. I supervise a lot of people.		
6. I have sufficient opportunities to persuade others to adopt my point of view.		
7. I have good contacts with people who can help me influence others.		
8. Influencing the way others behave is what my job is all about.		
TOTAL		

31 points or more

You like predictability in others and are good at getting things done. You tend to be a short cutter and people working with you may feel intimidated. You tend to want control over as many aspects of a role as possible. Many times you might manage by information control. There is a potential to become obsessed with influence. Your image is often involved in your administrative behavior.

30 to 23 points

You may hoard information, but can tolerate more irregularities in the behavior of others. There is a tendency to swing between the need for much power to no power, depending on the situation. You may be interested in the political aspects of your job. You can relinquish power when it is feasible.

22 or fewer points

You tend to be less threatening and more open to feedback. Also, you are better able to use the power of your title when needed. You tend to understand power but elect not to use it constantly.

If power is your primary trait in interactions and you are in a principal's role of negotiating with an advisory group, belonging behaviors might be more appropriate. Yet, you will probably sense the need to make a power move. What if you are high achievement-oriented, but that trait is constantly blocked because of organizational red tape or a power-based superintendent? Become aware that these motivational forces within us can be controlled and used at the proper times and in the situations where that trait enhances chances for success.

The tolerance assessment, the amount of hostility, and the motivational aspects are forces that can often be assessed as a cluster. This cluster often comes into play when a principal is backed into a corner. Be extra sensitive to your assessed traits because effective leaders monitor their behavior and are in control of the forces within them.

As the profiles are analyzed, do you begin to see a picture of the forces within you unfold? How do you fit into your own image as a leader?

Group Leadership

The forces within you emerge as you meet short-term tasks such as coordinating a task force for the district.

These three aspects of motivation—achievement, belonging, and power—represent the major leadership orientations since the early 1920s: task-oriented leadership, followed by relationship-oriented leadership in the 1940s, and more recently by situational styles of leadership.

Each of the orientations is associated with a particular motivational need. The high power need in a person relates to the situational or political style. The person high in belonging needs tends to do well in relationship leader roles, while the achievement need correlates highly with task orientation.

Another self-assessment profile generates information about a leader's approach to tasks.

Leadership Behavior: Exercise #6

The following items describe aspects of leadership behavior. Respond to each item according to the way you would be most likely to act if you were the leader of a work group designing a program for phasing in women's sports programs in a predominately blue collar district. Circle whether you would be likely to behave in the described way always (A), frequently (F), occasionally (O), seldom (S), or never (N).

If I were the leader of a work group . . .

A F O S N	1.	I would most likely act as the spokesperson of the group.
A F O S N	2.	I would allow members complete freedom in their work.
A F O S N	3.	I would encourage the use of uniform procedures.
A F O S N	4,	I would permit the members to use their own judgment in solving problems.
A F O S N	5.	I would needle members for greater effort.
A F O S N	6.	I would let the members do their work the way they think best.
A F O S N	7.	I would keep the work moving at a rapid pace.
A F O S N	8.	I would turn the members loose on a job, and let them go to it.
A F O S N	9.	I would settle conflicts when they occur in the group.
A F O S N	10.	I would be reluctant to allow the members any freedom of action.
A F O S N	11.	I would decide what shall be done and how it shall be done.
A F O S N	12.	I would push for increased production.
A F O S N	13.	I would assign group members to particular tasks.
A F O S N	14.	I would be willing to make changes.
A F O S N	15.	I would schedule the work to be done.
A F O S N	16.	I would refuse to explain my actions.
A F O S N	17.	I would persuade others that my ideas are to their advantage.
A F O S N	18.	I would permit the group to set its own pace.

T _____   P _____

Score your responses as follows:
- Circle the item number for items 1, 3, 9, 10, 11, 15, 16, and 17.
- Write a "1" in front of the circled items to which you responded S (seldom) or N (never).
- Write a "1" in front of items not circled to which you responded A (always) or F (frequently).
- Circle the "1's" which you have written in front of the following items: 2, 4, 5, 6, 8, 10, 14, 16, and 18.
- Count the circled "1's." This is your score for *concern for people.* Record the score in the blank following the letter "P" at the end of the questionnaire.
- Count the uncircled "1's." This is your score for *concern for production.* Record this number in the blank following the letter "T."

In order to locate yourself on the Managerial Grid below, find your score for *Concern for Production* on the horizontal axis of the Grid. Next, move up the column corresponding to your *Production* score to the point of intersection with your *Concern for People* score. Place an "X" at the intersection that represents your two scores. Numbers in parentheses correspond to the major styles on the Managerial Grid.

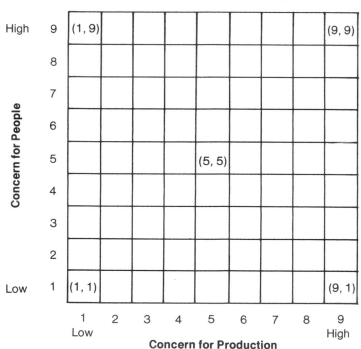

21

TASK MANAGER (9, 1)

The task manager has nine degrees of concern for production and only one degree of concern for people. In other words, the manager who has a 9,1 style is primarily concerned with output and sees his central responsibility as that of achieving production objectives. Similar to machines, people are seen as tools of production. They are paid to do what they are told, when they are told, and how they are told and not to ask too many questions in between. To question their superior is equal to insubordination. When interpersonal conflict arises, the task manager handles it through disciplinary action. Under task management, if people do not comply after a certain amount of control has been applied, they will be replaced.

COUNTRY CLUB MANAGER (1,9)

In contrast to the task manager, the country club manager has only one degree of concern for production but nine degrees of concern for people. His assumption is that if people are kept happy and harmony is maintained, a reasonable amount of productivity will be achieved. In short, people are pretty much like cows and if you keep them contented they will produce. If human problems and conflicts arise, they are glossed over or ignored. If the country club manager is asked "What is your primary responsibility?" he would most likely answer "To keep people happy." When employed to its extreme, the people who work for the 1,9 manager will usually sense a phony quality in human relations because they are not related to the conditions of work and production. Thus, long-run meaningful human relations are not achieved in the organization.

IMPOVERISHED MANAGER (1,1)

The manager in this position de-emphasizes concern for production and does just enough to get by. He also disregards the importance of human relationships. More directly, the impoverished manager is going nowhere and trying to take everybody with him. For all practical purposes he has retired, although he may be around for several more years. An impoverished management orientation may be found in circumstances where a person has been repeatedly passed over for promotion or feels he has otherwise been unjustly treated. Rather than looking elsewhere, he adjusts by giving minimal performance. Obviously, if the organization had too many 1,1 managers it would disappear.

DAMPENED PENDULUM MANAGER (5,5)

Push enough to get acceptable production but yield to the degree necessary to develop morale is the theory behind dampened pendulum or middle-of-the-road management. The 5,5 manager constantly shifts between his emphasis and concern for production and people. It represents a "live and let live" approach under which the real issues are muted. Most dampened pendulum managers are basically task managers at heart, but they read a book or went to a training seminar and learned that you cannot ride roughshod over people, so they have adopted a compromise approach. The point is, however, that they have missed the real issue.

TEAM MANAGER (9,9)

The team manager believes that a situation may be created whereby people can best satisfy their needs and objectives by working toward the objectives of the organization. He seeks to integrate people around production. When a problem arises, the team manager will meet with his group, present the situation, encourage discussion, and get ideas and commitment. He will delegate responsibility and give his people some freedom to operate. When emotional problems arise in working relationships, the team manager will confront them directly and work through the differences.

QUICK QUIZ

Decision making is one of the most important of the manager's functions. Each of the following statements characterizes the decision-making approach of one of the five managerial styles just discussed. Indicate the position (9,1; 1,9; 1,1; 5,5; or 9,9) of each on the Managerial Grid.

1. Anxious to make decisions which reflect the opinions of others so that the decisions will be accepted. Outer directed. _____
2. Decisions tend to obscure real issues. _____
3. Decisions are developed with the aid of those who have relevant facts and knowledge to contribute. _____
4. Depends on own skills and beliefs when making decisions. Inner directed. _____
5. Decisions are avoided or deferred to others for action. _____

OBSERVATIONS ABOUT THE MANAGERIAL GRID

Although the four corners and the midpoint of the grid are emphasized, these extreme positions are rarely found in their pure form in a working situation. In other words, a manager would more likely have a style of 8,3 or 4,6 or a similar combination.

In their research on the grid, Blake and Mouton have found that managers tend to have one dominant style which they use more often than any other. In addition, they have a backup style which is adopted if the dominant style does not work in a particular situation. For example, managers with 9,1 orientations who find that subordinates will not submit to their authority may have a 5,5 backup style. Similarly, 1,9 managers attempt to keep people happy and forestall interpersonal conflict; however, if this does not work, they may retreat and move in a 1,1 direction.

Another research finding is that the styles that individual managers choose as being best descriptive of themselves are very often not the way they really are. Rather, the choices reflect how they would like to be or how they would like to think their subordinates see them. Their second choices usually give a better reflection of how they really manage.

The ingredients of each managerial style are found to some degree in every manager. Managers' styles will be influenced by any number of factors, including their superiors, the kind of people they supervise, the situations in which they find themselves, and their own personalities. Although the obvious suggestion is that the closer a manager can come to a 9,9 style the better, it should also be noted that there is no one style that works best in all situations and with all people.

BLAKE AND MOUTON MANAGERIAL GRID

1,1	Little concern for either production or people.	The Deserter type	Worst leadership style.
1,9	Lowest concern for production, highest concern for people.	Missionary type	People-oriented style.
9,1	Highest concern for production, lowest for people.	The Autocrat type	Production-oriented style.
5,5	Comfortable concern for both production and people.	The Compromiser type	Maintain present balance style.
9,9	Highest concern for both production and people.	The Executive type.	Peak of leadership style.

Consequences	1,1	1,9	5,5	9,1	9,9
Basis for Boss-Subordinate Coordination	Acquiescence	Dependence	Consent	Compliance	Consensus
Subordinate Reactions	Going all out, leaving, apathy	Security; resentment and frustration, stifled creativity, leaving	Like begets like, "statistical" 5,5 drifting into 1,1	Fighting back resentful, anti-organization creativity; passive-compliance, hiding and for-getting escape	"Can do" spirit, "it's too much to ask . . . it's impractical."
Organization Characteristics	Bankrupt, care-taker situation	Welfare state orientation, country club	Bureaucracy, establishment "politics"	Command structure, reinforced by inspection	Functional, dynamic, purposeful
Long-Term Organization Implications	Drift towards actual bank-ruptcy	High expense, low production	Average production	Good production, short run	High production and return on investment

	1,1	1,9	5,5	9,1	9,9
Career Success	5th, poorest	4th, next to poorest	3rd or 2nd best	2nd and 3rd best	1st best
Mental	Emotional resignation	Masochism	Excessive worry	Sadism	Good spirits, respect and admiration
Physical	TB, cancer, "premature" death	Asthma, diabetes, hypertension (with 9,1 backup)	Peptic ulcer	Heart attack, migrane	Good health
Childhood Origins	Extreme coerciveness, deprivation and neglect, inconsistent expectations; complete indulgence.	Close direction provided with obedience rewarded; rejection with little or no approval given.	Emphasis on being "popular" and living up to expectations of one's peers.	Achievement demanded but is never "enough"; relative deprivation, partial pampering with disobedience punished.	Parents have a systematic model of development; unconditional love with cooperative parent/child activities, autonomy for actions with limits.

The incompleteness and imperfection of school organizations make overwhelming demands on the principal, who becomes the "hot seat person" to provide for the bulk of the responses to unforeseen or uncontrollable contingencies. Leaders must really know the forces within them as they go about their business of dealing with the human issues that continually arise in the world of public sector administration.

The school is one of the most public places. Public roles tend to magnify our internal views. Any time we go beyond policy and mechanical and rote compliance with school directives, we must be aware of the forces within those being led.

3. Forces Within Those Being Led

WHEN YOU ASK followers to be led, first be sure you are certain what it is you want. If you are unclear about the main objectives, the chances are the followers will be too. But beyond clarity in goal setting is the ability of the leader to know the forces operating within those being led. It is also important to be aware of the developmental growth within groups in general.

In public administrative roles we often bring units, task forces, curriculum advisory groups, etc., together to work as teams. One major operating force is based in the groups' feelings about team work. When people realize they are part of a team working toward a common goal, they are less apt to let their other team members down.

Prior to assessment of staff feelings about team work, you should be aware of the developmental forces within groups. These forces have definite stages.

The Developmental Forces Within Groups

Every group has to spend time and energy *learning* how to work together. It takes time for members, each different, to learn how they can fit into the group and contribute best. Often things seem "all mixed up," and group members may quite naturally become disturbed and discouraged—even aggravated at each other. These are natural "growing pains" of democratic groups, and tend to follow a predictable cycle or sequence. In most cases the group will become productive and efficient as people work to solve group problems.

Let's take a look at the stages in this developmental process.

1. *"Groping":* When the group is first finding out how to plan and work together they may not all agree. They don't know and understand each other well enough to really trust the others, and they still have to determine each others' skills, knowledge, situation and attitudes. They often feel uncomfortable and "lost."

2. *"Griping":* The members become discouraged when they can't seem to work together, when there isn't much progress, and their attempts are frustrated. They say the wrong things, play negative roles, and block group action because they are uncomfortable. This is the place for more "self-other" understanding, for remembering that they are all different but that they all want to do a good job and to be liked by others. Maybe they can learn to understand why others are griping, and learn to give themselves time to work things out.

3. *"Grasping":* Ideas and suggestions are beginning to fit. Members begin to agree and can start to see some direction to group activity. Everyone begins to feel more comfortable. Now they are getting somewhere.

4. *"Grouping":* Members are getting to know each other, and can understand and enjoy how each person works and fits into the scheme. Group tasks, building and maintenance roles come into play, and a surge of enthusiasm spreads through the group.

5. *"Group Action":* Now the group is in full swing, with members playing constructive roles. Leadership is shared and everyone is participating. It was difficult at first, but worth it to learn to work well together. They have shared in making plans and decisions, have learned together, and feel this is a good group with which to work. They are busy making their group more democratic.

Now they are ready to tackle other jobs. They will still go through some of these early stages, but each time it can be less disturbing and more effective.

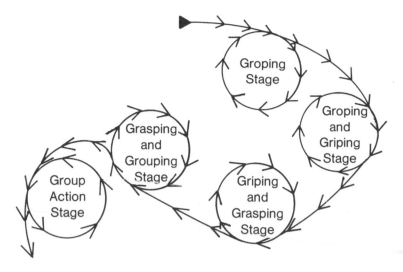

So it is important to recognize *how* members feel about each other; to know that these feelings are *natural* whenever they really tackle important jobs; to realize that the group can move ahead toward better relations between members. As they get to know each other better, this group gradually becomes *their* group because they have shared plans and work, and have tried to practice being cooperative, considerate, friendly, and democratic.

Team Behavior

The higher we go in an agency the more dependent we become on others. The following assessments are designed to give you insights about the forces within your followers in relationship to team work.

Team Building: Exercise #7

The 10 questions below are designed to assess your attitude toward various aspects of team building and to stimulate your thinking and group discussion about them. There obviously are no "right" or "wrong" answers to the questions.

For each item, circle the *one* number which best expresses how you feel.

	Strongly Opposed	Disagree	Undecided	Agree	Strongly Agree
1. Group work proceeds best when all group members speak freely or level with each other, as opposed to sparring or hiding opinions or feelings	1	2	3	4	5
2. An effective group faces up to and encourages disagreement, as opposed to smothering indifference	1	2	3	4	5
3. Strong feelings—including anger—if expressed will aid group work in the long run	1	2	3	4	5
4. It is important that decisions be made by talking things through—achieving consensus rather than voting or accepting a decision by the boss	1	2	3	4	5
5. An effective group gives support, recognition, encouragement, and earned praise to group members easily and freely	1	2	3	4	5
6. Silent members should be drawn into discussions so that everyone's ideas are secured and no one feels left out	1	2	3	4	5
7. It is important that group work contribute to all members feeling good about themselves and one another	1	2	3	4	5

	Strongly Opposed	Disagree	Undecided	Agree	Strongly Agree
8. Leadership roles (e.g., initiating, clarifying, summarizing) should be shared among the group so that all grow from group experience	1	2	3	4	5
9. "Feedback" to group members should be given freely so people will know when they are helping or hurting the group's progress	1	2	3	4	5
10. An effective group should stop the action now and then and evaluate its own functioning	1	2	3	4	5

The Personal Agenda: Exercise #8

The personal agenda gives all members the opportunity to speak to the entire group about their concerns and priorities. Most people *do* talk . . . to hear themselves. This process gives them a *license* to talk . . . and they enjoy it! It is an effective tool to determine the interests of the members. It gives everybody the experience of discovering the items that have high priority among the entire membership.

1. Each person will be given the opportunity to do ONE of three things:

   • *Ask a question to get factual information.* For example: "Where can I buy a good book on negotiation skills in this town?"

   • *Ask for help in solving a problem.* For example: "I have a staff member who always is late, and I need to know how to deal with that person."

   • *Make a statement.* For example: "I think we are ignoring the needs of new members and I, for one, would like to hear their ideas."

Participants must choose to do only ONE of the above and they should be given only one or two minutes in which to pose their question, or make their statement, and receive feedback from the group.

When the group begins giving feedback, individuals should be prepared to take notes on the information or help they receive.

2. Begin with any person who is ready with an item, and call "time" at the end of each person's time.

3. Repeat the process until everyone in the group has had an opportunity to speak.

The personal agenda gives everyone in the group two good experiences: being helped by others in the group; and helping others by sharing information which the others may not have had access to or experience with. And it gives the leaders a chance to really listen to those issues that are of major concern to the general membership.

When there is a need to assess additional and more pinpointed forces within the group, pass out "Questions for Staff. . . Pin Pointing" to each group member and have them complete the top portion. Then discuss the bottom half of the sheet.

Questions For Staff . . . . . . Pin Pointing

- Report a time when you felt either exceptionally good or exceptionally bad about an event that occurred on the job. The focus is to put on the specific event leading to the change in your attitude.

  What took place?

  Exceptionally good _____ _____

  Exceptionally bad _____ _____

- -

- Did you as a group hear any factor that is the most common dissatisfier or satisfier (frequency is a key)?

Also survey the group privately by sending out the Personal Survey Form with a pre-addressed, stamped envelope marked, "Principal (Personal)."

Personal Survey

1. The people in the school who make me feel the best are those who _____

2. The most important factor affecting morale at work is _____

3. The greatest satisfaction I get from my job is_____

4. If I could make one change in my work, it would be to _____

5. Our staff meetings are usually _____

6. The most irritating part of my job is _____

7. When something at work really aggravates me, I usually _____

8. When I can't get any help with my problems within the department, I usually turn to _____

The leaders who have used this technique find Item #8 responses give them insights about potential natural leaders in their buildings. A number of leaders find Item #5 to be beneficial in terms of feedback that is needed but is seldom received. Use the tool as a means of gaining insights about the forces within your school faculty as well as within other staff members. When conflict areas are noted or when major issues surface, the principal may wish to use the method below.

Strategies of Creative Conflict

When there is "conflict" in a group—that is, a lack of democratic behavior between two or more group members—it is usually "somebody" rather than an "idea" that is under attack. In other words, people tend to say, "I don't agree with YOU," or "I think YOU are wrong," instead of "I don't agree with your IDEA," or "I think the IDEA you have placed before the group lacks merit."

Here are some things to keep in mind when dealing with a conflict situation.

1. *Understand yourself and others.*
   - Interpret your feelings—don't explode them.
   - Try to understand the other's situation, and point of view.
   - Try to get a "third-person" viewpoint, to see the situation objectively.

2. *Keep improving your skill and power to express your position and feeling.*
   - People know and understand you by what you do and say, not by what you "mean."
   - Watch what words you use. Do the words mean the same thing to both or all of you? An argument is often no more than a misunderstanding.
   - Work to communicate your real self and yet keep up the lines of communication.
   - Do not destructively attack the "self-concept" of the other person.

3. *Get at the causes of the conflict, don't just look at the symptoms.*

4. *Be unto each other as persons—respect each other and trust each other.*

Detach your leadership role from the assessment of the forces within your followership group. Have each team member complete the Management of Interpersonal Conflict form. This allows those led to provide some clarity to their view of a problem, and as a form of self enlightenment for team members, usually assists the group process.

As a group, discuss items 2a, 2b and 2e. Discuss Item 10 to assess the group's strong points or talents.

Management Of Interpersonal Conflict: Exercise #9

1. Describe a *present* interpersonal conflict you must manage: _____

_____

_____

_____

_____

2. Is this conflict between:

    (a) Your goals and his?*
    (b) Your differing approaches to the same goal
    (c) Your needs and his?
    (d) Your values and his?
    (e) Differing role expectations?

3. Elaborate on Question 2. (For example, what is his goal and what is yours?) _____

_____

4. List *all* possible ways in which you might manage this conflict. I could:

    (a) _____
    (b) _____
    (c) _____
    (d) _____
    (e) _____
    (f) _____
    (g) _____
    (h) _____

5. Consider each of the alternatives you have listed above in terms of your "opponent's" most likely reaction.

    If I: He would:

6. Considering his probable responses, which alternatives would satisfy both of you? _____

_____

*the gender is only illustrative of the process

7. Can you adapt this solution in any way so it can satisfy both of you more fully? _____
_____

8. Previously, you considered his probable reaction to this solution. How can you help him react more positively? _____
_____
_____
_____

9. Assuming that this solution does not wholly satisfy your own needs, *how else* might you satisfy these needs? _____
_____
_____
_____

10. List the strengths you possess which might help you in putting this alternative into action.
   1. _____
   2. _____
   3. _____
   4. _____
   5. _____

Frequently, the pressures principals work under are a function of their own devising, a troubling perception conjured up from within the self.

Find out what you are fighting or opposing or worrying about so you may choose the appropriate leadership techniques for the situation. Identify the forces within those being led, and find out if the forces are real for you. As you begin to take responsibility for your own role in selecting what you will respond to and determining what to do with your reactions, you can take greater charge of your administrative position. This will also help you tune into the forces within the groups you lead as well as service.

Listening to yourself enables you to take charge of your own patterns of personal growth, and to some extent, building growth. If in times of impending crises you see yourself as power-seeking, you can take the opportunity to change and make your leadership relations progress.

By taking responsibility for your own behavior, the distinction between your responses and other people's will become clearer. This requires mastery of the forces within yourself, your own inclinations to respond automatically to the demands and forces within the followers out of a sense of powerlessness, obligations, or a misplaced sense of responsibility.

The more carefully and clearly you listen to the forces, the better able you will be to modify your responses to change, to avoid conflict, and to guide your own staff or team to improved relationships. Focusing on what you can do, you will be able to reduce your anxiety, your uncertainty, and your vulnerability to negative external pressures. Change then can be a positive aspect of leadership and a chance for renewal.

The next section will focus on things somewhat removed, but directly related to our leadership roles, including forces within the broader environment at the system and cultural level.

4. Forces Within the System Environment

EVERY EDUCATIONAL SYSTEM, building, or district has two organizations: formal and informal.

The formal organization can be charted easily, and is clearly understood by outsiders. The informal organization is rarely available in written form, creates the bulk of the forces we must assess and respond to in a system, and consists primarily of norms carried on in the name of habit, tradition, social safety or expectation. In reality, it is what people actually *do* rather than what the district's public relations *say*.

These invisible or shadow organizations remain largely unavailable for concise examination. However, we as leaders need to assess the norms in this shadow organization if we are to be effective. Norms in a school system pass from one level of leadership to another. Administrators learn these norms from what the district lives rather than from what the emerging principals are taught. Indeed, the things they observe and learn are frequently in direct conflict with what appears in texts and training programs. These become unwritten rules or norms that guide an agency, whether or not the staffs and principals want them.

The norms in many districts cluster around four categories:

District, building, and individual pride. Often teachers or administrators speak of their schools or districts in a manner that clearly reflects pride. If there is a negative response to this norm, phrases and attitudes convey "I am only a building principal there."

Achievement and improvement. Districts which are positive in this norm reflect a success orientation. Those negative in this category accept the mediocre or routine.

Upward, downward, and sideward communications. The positive reflection is apparent in people at all levels who originate as well as respond to ideas and opinions. The "cover your lower anatomy" mentality is the negative norm. Unnecessary competition between departments and classes often indicates lack of this category of open communication.

Innovation and change. In this school you get positive strokes for new ideas. The negative view is that it doesn't pay to rock the boat in this building.

The norm analysis technique examines these categories and others in your building or district. This sample illustrates the process.

Norm Analysis: Exercise #10

A	B	C	D	E
Approve and encourage it	Approve but do nothing to encourage it	Consider it not worth their time	Disagree but take no action	Actively discourage it

If a teacher in your building (district) were to:

Most teachers would:

NOTE: Check only one per item

		A	B	C	D	E
1.	Come to school drunk	—	—	—	—	—
2.	Smoke pot when the students won't see the act.	—	—	—	—	—
3.	Fail to show up at class because of drug use.	—	—	—	—	—
4.	Talk about the drug problem with that teacher.	—	—	—	—	—

Assess your building personnel's responses for items such as inservice, teacher's aides, curriculum innovation, etc. Once we determine the norms operative in our building we start to understand the current forces within the district. If the norm is counterproductive to our view of the school's role then we can bring group pressure to focus on the change.

Also required for changes in system norms is central office/board commitment through resources made available; and through *actual behavior,* not P.R. statements of intent. If support cannot be obtained above the building level, present your findings to your staff, department by department. They probably will develop practical solutions. You may wish to re-use the team building assessment technique as a facilitation tool.

Another norming tool is the School Messages Technique.

School Messages: Exercise #11

The purpose of the exercises on scripts is not to do an in-depth personal survey but to begin to understand how scripts are formed and acted out in your building.

What might teachers say about:

doing work _____	using audiovisual equipment ____
getting educated _____	being a man _____
being religious _____	being a woman _____
achieving success _____	being good or bad _____
having brains _____	developing talents _____
attending workshops _____	being a good student _____

Analysis Worksheet: Exercise #12

The norms operative in your building often differ from the public statements about the functions and Central Office support for them. Have each person per department complete this worksheet so you may assess a norm. Optional are school-wide, department-wide, or district-wide norm surveying. Indicate with an "x" the importance *you* attach to each function.

FUNCTIONS	Most 9	8	7	6	5	4	3	2	Least 1
Communication									
Coordination									
Costs									
Clients									
Community									
Equipment/Facilities									
Morale									
Performance									
Planning									
Policies and Procedures									
Quality									
Self Development									
Contribution to Profession									
Work Assignments									
Interpersonal									
TOTAL = Care Level									

Importance

Leadership Norms

The system forces depend on the norms the top leaders and board members have regarding the nature of people. The X and Y theory developed by McGregor states two views of people. These aid in the assessment of top leadership norms. Ask your teachers to respond to the two following lists, noting the number of administrators and board members they feel hold each of the views.

The Assumptions of Theory X

_____ 1. The average human being has an inherent dislike of work and will avoid it if he can.

_____ 2. Because of this human characteristic—dislike of work— most people must be coerced, controlled, directed, threatened with punishment to get them to put forth adequate effort toward the achievement of organizational objectives.

_____ 3. The average human being prefers to be directed, wishes to avoid responsibility, has relatively little ambition, wants security above all.

The Assumptions of Theory Y

_____ 1. The expenditure of physical and mental effort in work is as natural as play or rest.

_____ 2. External control and the threat of punishment are not the only means for bringing about effort toward organizational objectives. Man will exercise self-direction and self-control in the service of objectives to which he is committed.

_____ 3. Commitment to objectives is a function of the rewards associated with their achievement.

_____ 4. The average human being learns, under proper conditions, not only to accept but to seek responsibility.

_____ 5. The capacity to exercise a relatively high degree of imagination, ingenuity, and creativity in the solution of organizational problems is widely, not narrowly, distributed in the population.

_____ 6. Under the conditions of modern industrial life the intellectual potentialities of the average human being are only partially utilized.

You can readily see that people holding Theory X assumptions would prefer an autocratic leader, whereas people holding Theory Y assumptions would prefer a more participative leadership style. The situation, however, might call for a different approach. For example, Theory Y principals might prefer to use close supervision with new employees and gradually evolve to a more participative style as the staff becomes more skilled and competent.

People, Careers, Rewards

Other forces evolve around the type of person the system may reward at different positions. There are numerous schemes for classifying people. This particular one may be useful in dealing with the reward system in your district.

Briefly, there are four major types of people in this scheme:

The *linear* type, who selects a career early in life, develops an upward path and carries it out, is exemplified by teacher→ principal→superintendent.

The *steady-state* person chooses a job area early, stays with it for life, and would be typified by a person who spends 40 years as a doctor, teacher or government clerk.

The *spiral* person stays in one area for five to seven years and then moves into another related career area. This person may start as a teacher then later get a counseling degree and work in the mental health field.

The *transitory* type is a job hopper—often a paid trouble shooter or a consultant. Other transitory people enter at the lower end of the pay scale, and to them the district job is only for income. Their true love may be tennis or skiing or real estate sales.

Reward systems differ to meet the needs of each particular type of person. The reward system designed to hold and encourage linear people must allow for rapid achievement and success. The reward system for steady-state people would include protected job boundaries with security from outside forces. Spiral people have much nervous energy and the system that rewards them allows for multiple moves within the framework of the district.

What type of person prevails in your faculty and staff? Which type is really rewarded? List the four trouble makers and the four joy givers on your faculty and other staff. Is there a common type in either list? Use this to assess the reward system at work. Again it is not that which is on paper, but that which *is* that affects leadership.

These four types of people also emerge as career types and Don Driver summarized them as follows:

- LINEAR people choose their career fields early, develop plans for upward movement in their fields, and carry them out.

  Linear workers are competitive, ambitious, aggressive, energetic, and have high self-esteem. They are skillful at office politics and know how to manipulate the rules to their advantage. "The linear tend to have a strong need for achievement, power and wealth . . . .They achieve to get noticed."

- STEADY-STATE people choose their career fields early, and stay with them for life, with no grand plans for advancement. Often, however, these people attain rising incomes and increase their professional skills.

  Steady-state people seek security and strong job boundaries. Most do not have strong needs for achievement, wealth, or power. Career government service is a classic example of a steady-state career path. "They receive little intrinsic job satisfaction."

  But, many professionals and craftsmen also follow a steady-state path. "There are many steady-state physicians, lawyers, and teachers who, I'm sure, enjoy their jobs." One example is attorney F. Lee Bailey.

- SPIRAL CAREER is really several careers. These people work in one area for a time, then move to a related field or sometimes to a totally different field. They frequently make their moves at five-to-seven year intervals.

  Spiral people have high self-esteem and strong needs for challenge, personal growth, fulfillment, and development. They seek achievement for its own sake and enjoyment.

Spirals tend to possess a lot of nervous energy and get real satisfaction from their jobs. "For these people, there is no difference between work and play. Play is work. Work is play. And that is why they put in such long hours."

The spiral career path is largely a modern day phenomenon, although history has seen its share of spirals—Michaelangelo, Ben Franklin, and Thomas Jefferson among them.

- TRANSITORY people job hop. Many are low-income drifters; others are well-paid "trouble shooters."

Transitory people are divided into two categories: Transitory 1 and Transitory 2.

Transitory 1 people are well-directed. They have great energy, high self-esteem, and possess strong needs for achievement, recognition, and challenge.

"They enjoy work a lot, but they have a high boredom level. These people go from job to job, challenge to challenge. They are known as turn-around people. Once they are at the point where things are running smoothly—or about to—they move on to a new challenge." Paul "Red" Adair, the legendary fighter of oil-well fires, is one example.

A Transitory 2 person possesses little self-esteem, energy, or self-direction. "They have trouble deciding what they want. They hope by changing jobs they will find out."

Frederick Herzberg developed another method for viewing the forces within the system which affect leadership. His theory suggests that job satisfaction and dissatisfaction are produced by different work factors. The context, invisible or shadow organizational factors, norms and reward systems, and under or over-loading of career types all are forces within the system effecting leadership.

The factors which make people satisfied with their work relate to the content of their jobs, such as achievement, recognition for achievement, interesting work, increased responsibility, growth, and advancement. These satisfiers are motivators, because if your district or school has them, your staff probably will have positive attitudes about their jobs.

On the other hand, the ways people are treated—not what they do—become the dissatisfier factors. These dissatisfiers—

specifically company policy, administrative practices, supervision, salary, status, and security—are all major factors. If the dissatisfiers are more prevalent, the forces at work in the staff probably will overshadow the bulk of the leadership work.

The principal can push central office policy to be as realistic as possible and focused on job satisfiers. A perceived gross injustice in the area of dissatisfiers can create a ripple that a building level principal may be unable to manage. When we can observe the needs of the followers, but do not have the power within the district to react to the needs, we, too, may feel the dissatisfaction.

An important influence in shaping the forces that make up our followership in schools is the all too-well-known Peter Principle. We may have vice-principals, supervisors, and others who are also in leadership roles in our building but are under our administrative control. Many of these people assume that because they occupy a supervisory role, they must be correspondingly strong, decisive, and self confident. It has been estimated that 75 percent of the population is notably passive, dependent, and submissive. Included in this estimate would be people elevated to the positions immediately below us.

We must, therefore, include high level building staff in our assessment. These types of second-level and mid-level administrative and supervisory people may take flight into detail or develop techniques that assure indefinite delay. They are also our followers. They are the system!

Other forces within the system might be assessed as skills available for success. Successful principals understand people and know how to get along with them. They are sensitive to the talents and feelings of others and know what to do or say in their relations with them.

The skills that help with system success include:

- sustaining or stick-to-it behavior;
- strong needs for achievement;
- positive images allowing for school experimentation;
- the ability of the staff to present themselves and thus the school;
- the ability to be in the right place at the right time to ward off disasters;

- informal public relations;
- competence.

These skills and talents are positive forces within the system. Diplomacy and tact are also helpful. Diplomacy reduces hostility and antagonism, and your ability to use tact by being slow to criticize and by showing a willingness to ask for help rubs off on others.

Power

The concept of power pervades all organizational relationships. The nature and uses of power, however, have been studied more often as historical or political struggles than as conflicts among people and organizations. It is important to understand power as a dynamic element of human behavior in organizations and as a force within the staff.

Educational organizations are not immune to the interplay of power's forces. This concept seems contrary to the idea of organizations being devoted to schooling, stimulation and democracy; yet even the student and the family are part of the power system. The interaction of people in any setting includes the subtleties of power; therefore, power is inevitably present in the system at the building level. This section analyzes the power system that energizes the work of administrators, and examines the administrator's role in the organization with respect to the power problems it entails.

To many professionals "power" is an undesirable word, connoting dominance and submission, control and acquiescence, or one person's will over another's. Some even go so far as to state that anyone interested in power is sick, and that the interests of "political man" result from the displacement of private conflicts into public issues.

To others, however, leadership *is* the exercise of power, and it is dangerous and misleading to equate the need for power with illness. Working from a psychoanalytical framework, power-oriented behavior can be viewed in the context of total personality development and character structure, with power having both normal and pathological expressions. Power, like any human attribute, can be benevolent or malicious, used or abused, inspiring or stifling, but it is a force within most systems.

Power is defined as one person's degree of influence over others to the extent that obedience or conformity follow. There is little or no question of acquiescence. Only the most indifferent or rebellious will fail to carry out the demands of a power figure. Acquiescence is essential and, when genuine, makes power a legitimate form of influence over the work behavior of organization members.

A second legitimating influence which supports the use of power in organizations is properly delegated authority. Power and authority are thus closely coupled forms of influence which together make the organization coherent and move it toward achieving its goals. Can outsiders sense how your system really functions?

Types of Power

Power derives from multiple sources which can operate simultaneously. *Legitimate power* is that authority vested in a role or office which is accepted and recognized by the members of the organization. *Reward power* is based on the administrator's use of positive sanctions. This may be as simple as a compliment or as complex as monetary benefits like summer teaching. *Coercive power* is the opposite of reward power and involves negative sanctions such as threats of harm, punishment, or witholding rewards. *Expert power* is founded on valid knowledge or information. *Referent power* is based on attractive personal characteristics which lead others to emulate or please the attractive person. All of these sources are legitimate and are available to the administrator.

Derivative forms are also useful to the administrator. For example, *associative power* comes from close alliance with a powerful individual or group. The staff and the administrative group are examples of associate power in the school. Another derivative form is *power of the lower participants of a hierarchy over the higher members*. For example, the school principal may have power over the central office administrator through 1) control of resources upon which the person is dependent; 2) control of the access of others to that person; 3) control of techniques, procedures or knowledge vital to the administrator; and 4) personality attributes such as charm, likeableness, or charisma recognized by the administrator as desirable in subordinates. Note that this same type of power can be utilized by staff members against the principal.

The results of derivative forms of power are more uncertain than other forms. Some derivative powers are more likely to be considered legitimate than others. Lay participants or other staff may circumvent or manipulate the organizational hierarchy by using various forms of power that are not legitimate. Also, a derivative power may be legitimate in some circumstances but not in others.

Assessing Power

Although there are other approaches to the study of power, we are just beginning to learn more about the role of personality and its uses in organizations. For example, the acquiescence to or acceptance of power implies submissiveness, docility, or the desire to be dominated. Yet in the organizational context, there are interesting countervailing forces; authority figures are often temporary and must therefore meet commonly held goals; and there are many forms of acquiescence and many ways to live with authority.

McClelland classifies power orientations into four stages according to the ego-development of the individual. The stages are not progressive; rather they represent alternative actions from which people achieve a feeling of power.

Stage I: "It" strengthens me.

Adults in this stage are infantile—still gaining strength from another person. They are totally dependent on others as their source of strength. Being a close associate of a powerful person is their preferred status.

Stage II: I strengthen myself.

Persons at this stage feel powerful through control of their bodies or possessions. They may embark on bodybuilding exercises or the acquisition of material possessions. They may feel in control through understanding what makes people tick or how systems operate.

Stage III: I have impact on others.

This stage is exemplified by feelings of power through controlling others. These persons are competitive, and may try to outwit or outmaneuver other people or may give things to others in order to control or dominate.

Stage IV: "It" moves me to do my duty.

Persons in this stage may subordinate personal goals to a higher authority or make decisions based on the good of the organization. Power plays based on individual authority carry a far more dangerous potential than power plays based on organizational authority.

Power and the Administrator

Awareness of the sources, uses, and abuses of power is vital to the astute administrator, yet some are reluctant to participate in a game that goes by the rules of power. It is an asset to be able to play the game with consummate skill, but to shun power entirely is to be a weak and ineffective leader. Those without power or the willingness to use it risk losing the confidence and respect of subordinates. True, it is helpful to wear the mantle of power lightly, to use it sparingly, and to remain cautious in its demonstration. The principal must come to terms with conflicts between personality, professional ideals, and the needs of the building.

The building administrator's position and title signify legitimate power and authority generally recognized throughout the organization. There may be a disagreement as to the precise scope of this power and authority, but it is usually adequate for solving problems within an individual department. Beyond the department itself, this is not always the case, for the department is more homogeneous and coherent than are the parts of an organization viewed as a whole. Again, we as administrators are part of the forces at play in the system. There is less danger of excessive reliance on one or a few of its available sources, or the use of power for its own sake.

Principals derive expert power from two sources: professional knowledge and administrative skill. But this duality poses an inner conflict, for the two types of expertise are not always compatible. Principals are not executives in the full sense, nor are they solely practicing professionals. Concomitantly they exercise influence in determining goals and policy, and in directing the movement of their professional groups toward departmental and institutional goals.

The administrator may or may not be an attractive, professional person with enough referent power to be a model to others. Referent power is diminished when the administrator develops hostile, defensive personality patterns.

The principal has access to associative power through contacts with general administration and the central staff. Power really is a force within, and can be assessed. You cannot avoid this force, but you need not fear it.

Promotion concepts are forces within the system. In your district are you younger than or older than the others in your type of principalship? Are you aware of any pattern of promotion via the person's background? For example, which would be most preferred for principal in your district, a person from science, coaching, contemporary world problems, or an out-of-district person?

How long do people remain in the district prior to becoming a principal if they show that as a career goal? Did you make principal faster or more or less at the typical rate for your district? Are those factors that might be at play on the others in your building, if they aspire to leadership positions?

Role Factors

The last force within the system to be assessed is one which is best facilitated by use of the role factors chart.

Role Factors Chart

Factors effecting friend and partner selections and interactions between people, agencies, and institutions:

1. **Role Theory**
   STRESS: *"Can I live up to the role?"*
   Focus of attention is on behavior and attitudes appropriate to a situation irrespective of the individual.

2. **Needs Theory**
   STRESS: *"Will the role block my true needs?"*
   Focus is on behavior and attitudes that are characteristic of people irrespective of the situation but based on needs.

3. **Value Theory**
   STRESS: *"Is 'this' right to do?"*
   Focus is sharing similar evaluations of good/bad and other polarities.

4. **Exchange Theory** STRESS: *"What do they expect from me for their behavior?"*	Focus is on bargaining in a non direct way (exchange is at a low level or sub-conscious level of awareness).
5. **Sequential Theory** STRESS: *"What if I'm at level 4 and my (agency) partner is still hung up at the role level?"*	Focus is on developmental phasing of above four theories.

If your main reward in the system is to fit the role, then this becomes a force within the district. Teachers who "teach" to the needs of the students, may upset others with the noise and behavior these turned-on-students exhibit. If the teachers are cautioned, there is a good chance they violated the "role" view held in that building.

Each building seems to have its own forces, but as a principal the forces within your district that are related to this role factors chart become essential to assess. The stress created as a force within the building or system occurs when top leadership changes the major thrust from one category to another.

Stress may also be created if incoming professionals have norms different from the district's norm—for example, if the district norm of bureaucratic maintenance, primarily an exchange theory norm, is contested by new staff oriented toward confrontation and negotiation around their needs.

This chapter has focused on a number of the forces within a system, building or district in size. A typical problem of educational leaders is inaccurate insight coupled with false self assessment. We must view the system forces on broader bases. When assessed some factors may highlight the ever-so-slight deviations from established district practices that permit the principal to react from a realistic rather than a hoped-for base. The focus is on re-assessment of self-reinforcing actions which also can hinder leadership.

5. Forces Within the Individual

A NORM IN ALL leadership seminars is to demand that the individuals "know themselves." The self and the forces on the self in society are two different kinds of forces. The forces within the individual in the culture are needed as data for we who educate the emerging adult. As leaders, we are part of the culture.

Developing Self-Concepts

People take a view of their many selves early in life. From birth to about 8 years of age, children tend to please their parents and their parents' peers. From about third grade to ninth grade there is a strong drive to please their own peers. As adulthood develops, people learn to please their own talents, abilities and desires while monitoring the value of other's opinions and while assessing the culture. All influences and summations or conclusions about the influences in these earlier years make adult leaders what they are in their leadership roles.

The earliest influences upon the self-concept are the parents, who teach children their worth through the love and care lavished upon them . . . or denied to them. That children need to be loved for themselves goes almost without saying. No one would deny that love and care are most basic needs for an infant's healthy emotional growth. Although the effects of different practices in infant care are debatable (i.e., weaning, toilet training, etc.), the effects of parental attitudes are not. In fact, the *attitudes* of parents seem to be of greater consequence than their behavior. The attitudes of love and care, for example, satisfy the infant's needs, which, in turn, provide the security which enables the child to venture out into the world, engage in activities, and make contact with others. In a sense, the attitudes of love and care are the first affirmation of the child's worth. The parent says, in effect, "You're very important to me. You *should* be given love and care. You deserve it. You're worth taking care of . . . I value you."

The child's self-concept is greatly influenced by parental acceptance or rejection. Impressive research proves that institutionalized children—i.e., children denied this love and attention—do not develop "normally." Not only do they fail to develop their potential strengths, but they seem to *lose* "natural" strengths they may already possess. Without the rudiments of a positive self-concept, without this basic affirmation of worth, children seem to lose interest in themselves and the world. They "shrivel" into apathy and withdrawal. They lack the basic self-assurance required for venturing into, or mastering their world.

This basic parental affirmation can be seen as a nucleus around which the child's self concept will form. Yet love and care, essential as they are, are not the only requirements for development of a positive self-concept. Children must also become aware that they are unique *individuals* with special talents, abilities, preferences, interests, etc., and that they are *also* valued for these strengths. Through affirmation of their own unique strengths, children develop a sense of their own identities. They learn who they are.

We can say that children first learn to value themselves when they are valued by others—first by their parents and later by their environments. The parents affirm their children's worth through the love and care they give them. Later, both parents and the environment as a whole enhance and build upon these basic self concepts through appreciation and acceptance of the children's unique individual strengths.

Murial James summarized the effects of early childhood influences in terms of personal conclusions people develop about their worth and positioning in life.

When taking positions about themselves, people may conclude:

I do many things right.

I do everything wrong.

I don't deserve to live.

I'm as good as anybody else.

I can't think for myself.

I have a good head on my shoulders.

When taking positions about others, a person may conclude:

People are wonderful.

People are no damn good.

People will help me.

People are out to get me.

People can't be trusted.

People are basically honest.

The above positions can be generalized: "I'm OK" or "I'm not OK," and "You're OK" or "You're not OK." They fit together to form the four basic life positions.

The First Position: "I'm OK, You're OK" is potentially a mentally healthy position. If realistic, people with this position about themselves and others can solve their problems constructively. Their expectations are likely to be valid. They accept the significance of people.

The Second or Projective Position: "I'm OK, You're not OK" is the position of persons who feel victimized or persecuted. They blame others for their miseries. Delinquents and criminals often have this position and take on a paranoid behavior which in extreme cases may lead to homicide.

The Third or Introjective Position: "I'm not OK, You're OK" is a common position of persons who feel powerless when they compare themselves to others. This position leads them to withdraw, to experience depression, and, in severe cases, to become suicidal.

The Fourth or Futility Position: "I'm not OK, You're not OK" is the position of those who lose interest in living, who exhibit schizoid behavior, and in extreme cases, commit suicide and/or homicide.

56

The individual may also focus primarily on use of one or more defense mechanisms. The current culture has an above average amount of emotional insulation. This brief outline may point to your particular reaction in your leadership role. Keep in mind this defense system started prior to this job, and may be adaptive or maladaptive, depending on the circumstances and the rigidity of the defense.

Defense Mechanisms

Mechanism:	Function:
Compensation	Covering up weaknesses by emphasizing desirable trait or making up for frustration in one area by over-gratification in another.
Identification	Increasing feelings of worth by identifying with person or institution of illustrious standing.
Introjection	Incorporating external values and standards into ego structure so individual is not at their mercy as external threats.
Projection	Placing blame for difficulties upon others or attributing one's own unethical desires to others.
Rationalization	Attempting to prove that one's behavior is "rational" and justifiable and thus worthy of self and social approval.
Repression	Preventing painful or dangerous thoughts from entering consciousness.
Reaction Formation	Preventing dangerous desires from being expressed by exaggerating opposed attitudes and types of behavior and using them as "barriers."
Displacement	Discharging pent-up feelings, usually of hostility, on objects less dangerous than those which initially aroused the emotions.
Emotional Insulation	Withdrawing into passivity to protect self from hurt.
Isolation	Cutting off affective charge from hurtful situations or separating incompatible attitudes by logic-tight compartments.

Regression	Retreating to earlier developmental level involving less mature responses and usually a lower level of aspiration.
Sublimation	Gratifying frustrated sexual desires in substitute nonsexual activities.
Undoing	Atoning for and thus counteracting immoral desires and acts.

Maslow's Hierarchy

Each of us has individual deficit and growth needs. When an individual loses a chance at obtaining any of the growth, basic, or deficit needs, that person then is in a traumatic situation. Leadership at all levels is affected when the whole culture loses a basic need level. Recall the famous triangle of needs popularized by Maslow.

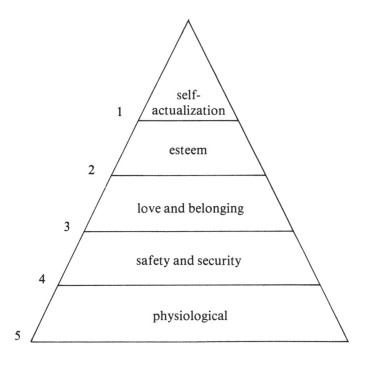

When the district's population changes, the forces motivating the lay public may differ widely from the norms operative in the system. We must then be able to assess our growth needs as well as those in the school attendance area.

LEVELS OF DEFICIT NEEDS

- *Physiological needs* are aimed at biological survival. The needs for food, water, rest, etc., recur throughout life. Cultural influences often determine the specific ways in which these needs are met.

- *Safety needs* are the needs for security, order, stability. These needs are active throughout life, but are seen most clearly in children.

- *Need for belongingness.* Everyone needs to interact with others in a way which proves that their actions do have an effect and make a difference to others. These are the needs to give and receive affection.

- *Esteem needs* are the needs for self-respect and recognition. What individuals think of themselves depends to a large degree on what others think of them.

LEVELS OF GROWTH NEEDS

According to Maslow, these are the most characteristically *human* needs.

- *Need for information* . . . to be acquainted with and at home with the facts of one's environment.

- *Need for understanding* . . . to discover patterns of existence, to correlate the facts of life. All people have this need, even if it must be supplied by a "witch doctor," who can "explain" things.

- *Need for beauty* . . . aesthetic experience. This is the only way to explain those elements in every culture which have no functional value whatever.

- *Need for self-actualization* . . . the need to fulfill one's potentialities . . . "Whatever a man can be, he must be if he is to be happy and healthy."

Because Maslow takes a different approach to motivation than do the other theorists considered, he also takes a different approach to strengths. Referring to his hierarchy of needs, we can see that as man fulfills needs on one level, he is free to move to a higher level, until he is able to devote most of his energy to such "higher needs" as information, understanding, beauty, and self-actualization. Leaders often reflect the culture, because after all they are a product of it.

Operative Values Within Me: Exercise #13

Part of the forces within the individual are created by the "should/ oughts" operating in their lives prior to the time when they had the power or the words to argue against or modify them. These "oughts" and "shoulds" emerge as operative values in the life of the individual. Complete your response to these questions for an assessment of operative values:

1. Here are the values I see operative in my building:

   _____,
   in my district _____,
   in our school board: _____,
   in this community in general: _____.

2. Here are the values I see operative in the principal's position in my building:_____
   _____

3. And, here are the values I see operative in my own personal out-of-the-school-world life: _____
   _____.

Should/Would Internal Assessment: Exercise #14

As an individual, you also have personal battles over other "oughts" and "shoulds." These are questions that you can respond to in terms of ought to or should not do, to assess this force within you as an individual. Therefore, respond as you would if you excluded the principalship title you hold. Then, respond as the building principal in a liberal district; then, as a principal in a conservative district.

Place an X in the column if it is deemed appropriate in your mind. S = Should W = Would	As Self		Liberal District		Conservative District	
	S	W	S	W	S	W
Moonlight 10 hours a week at a rate 3 times your current salary's hourly rate.						
Volunteer 5 hours every other week for Big Sister/Big Brother program for underprivileged and single parent children in your area.						
Attend a human potential growth seminar that your superintendent recommended.						
Give up a day of your summer vacation to hear an authority in your field discuss practical management concepts for school principals.						
Give up a day of school year vacation time to hear a seminar of new research on how high school students learn.						
Commit one weekend a month to teach Sunday School.						
Spend 5 hours per week during the evening hours seeking ways to influence legislation in your state.						
Stay up late to help a personal friend.						
Drink with the other district principals.						
Pay $10.00 a month for a fund to help children in another country.						
Continue with your education to the doctorate degree.						
Spend evenings and weekends on school work and projects.						

Do you feel you are that different from other individuals in professional roles in your geographical area?

Rollo May noted, "Every human being gets much of his sense of his own reality out of what others say to him and think about him. But, many modern people have gone so far in their dependence on others for their feeling of reality that they are afraid that without it they would lose the sense of their own existence." As leaders, we are in part our own experts, *but* we are indeed dependent upon others for awareness of the realities of our district and our building.

To be aware of forces within individuals in the society allows leaders to remain aware, yet not be so vulnerable to changing judgments about them that they become unpredictable. The ought/should/would type of analysis of forces helps administrators see the expectations or opinions of others, not make them withdrawn, apathetic or defiant. Principals must realize that they stabilize a district because school boards and superintendents may have an in-district life of less than 20 years.

At each stage in life the individual is faced with developmental tasks influencing future behavior. For example, if a woman marries at age 17, by the time she reaches 30 she may wish to rediscover her adolescent development and seek a divorce, not because of her husband but because of her lack of experiencing the adolescent development. People who have missed certain developmental stages may inappropriately try to recapture them when they are in leadership roles. People denied a chance to experience a developmental phase might strive to overcompensate when they reach adulthood.

Thus far, we have explored the forces within individuals in a culture, with a heavy emphasis on the interpersonal, intrapersonal, and need systems which influence their later behavior. Yet, obviously, neither self concept or self confidence are static, unchanging things. Both continue to grow and develop as the individual progresses through life and career.

An administrator is faced with career and job tasks which force the acquisition of new response patterns. The major positive force within an individual in a culture that can enhance later administrator success is the force focused on demands for flexibility. People who accept this, function in leadership roles. If, however, they polarize and want everything under their control, they become stressed and nonfunctional administrators.

The basic and continuing needs of people are forces within an individual that must be assessed from time to time. The two following assessment techniques have a common focus: the forces within the individual that are reflected in personal need and career need assessments.

Personal Needs: Exercise #15

Answer the following as they apply to the last six months.

A . . . Never   C . . . . Most of the time
B . . . Some of the time   D . . . . Always

THE PHYSICAL NEEDS: The basic survival needs for man allowing him to exist.

____ 1. My living quarters meet my physical needs.
____ 2. I eat what I need.
____ 3. My everyday surroundings are suitable.
____ 4. I am able to sleep easily.
____ 5. My sex life is satisfactory.

THE SAFETY NEEDS: The need for order and stability in a person's life.

____ 1. I feel secure.
____ 2. My life is smooth and consistent.
____ 3. People treat me fairly.
____ 4. My world is stable.
____ 5. I handle new situations comfortable.

THE AFFECTION NEEDS: The knowing you need to love and be loved.

____ 1. I trust those close to me.
____ 2. I am trusted by those close to me.
____ 3. I feel affection *for* those close to me.
____ 4. I feel affection *from* those close to me.
____ 5. I feel included.

THE ESTEEM NEEDS: The need to feel confident that what you do is recognized not only by yourself but also by others.

____ 1. I respect myself.
____ 2. I feel like a man/woman.
____ 3. Others feel I am a capable person.
____ 4. I have self confidence.
____ 5. I feel people respect me.

THE PERSONAL DEVELOPMENT NEEDS: The feeling one is becoming *everything* he is capable of becoming.

_____ 1. I am developing my potential abilities.
_____ 2. I have a drive to know and accept myself.
_____ 3. I feel happy.
_____ 4. I am becoming the person I want to be.
_____ 5. I experience moments of great joy.

Career Needs From Within

Achievement:

- Do I prefer to see the end of my work or am I content to work on one part of the process?
- Do I like doing fewer things very well, or many times do I prefer to rush through many things?
- Am I happiest when concentrating on one task at a time or when working on many projects going at the same time?
- Is it important that work lead to bigger opportunities or do I prefer limited responsibility?
- Do I get impatient with long range projects?

Challenge:

- Am I bored with easy work? Do I enjoy tackling difficult problems or would I rather have work that is easier on my nerves?
- Do I work well under pressure deadlines?
- Do I have the physical energy to survive a fast paced job?
- If someone tells me something can not be done, do I like to do it to prove it can be done?
- Do I feel unfulfilled unless I have challenging work?

Creativity:

- Would I be happy in a setting where superiors make all the decisions without asking for my ideas?
- Am I always thinking of original solutions or short cuts?

Dominance:

- Am I happy or unhappy if I am not running the show?
- Do I resent it when others question my authority or expertise?

Helping Others:

- Do I have a compulsion to do work that has meaning for others . . . to work for an individual's or society's benefit? What kind of people (children, sick people, powerless people, healthy, etc.) as clients?

- Would I be happier working in a service or non-profit agency than a commercial one?

This chapter focused on forces within an individual in the culture that later are reflected and help or hinder the leadership function. In the next chapter the forces within the culture in general will be explored.

6. Forces Within The Culture

IN THE LATE 1920s and 1930s there was a "Fix It" mind set. People tried to fix radios, cars, ice boxes, relationships, marriages; and work was oriented toward pride in quality. The job market was oriented toward making goods and services. The leader of that day "fixed" people to be able to fit in a situation if desired.

The Second World War and Korean War years brought in a "Replacement" mind set. Instead of fixing a radio, a person was taught how to replace a whole unit such as the audio circuit, and eventually, the whole radio. People replaced one another and divorce rates went up at an alarming rate. We had his or her towels, separate cars, double garages, separate checking accounts, all designed to make replacement easier than maintenance or repair. The focus was on making jobs, not products of worth.

The educational leaders, thus had to replace "knowledge fixing" with "replacement thinking." They had to replace books, replace techniques, and rotate teachers, rather than fix the situation and responsibility for learning. "Rosie the Riveter" replaced males in factories and child-rearing was replaced by television and a slew of government-funded "child helping" programs.

The "No Action" mind set evolved, and by the 1960s people were dropping out of competition, relationships, marriages, knowledge acquisition situations, and politics. Drugs became a way to ensure minimal responses because unions and pressure groups and automatic "passing" from grade to grade assured that no action on the part of the individual or the host agencies would really occur.

A stronger movement to foster an illusion of independence or self-reliance causes our society to mock the need for group or institutional responsibility. An enormous number of people now own enough "free" time to buy privacy, space, and isolation. This is reflected in learning by isolate and self-paced programmed interventions all the way to top administrators who rarely are in the buildings where students go to school.

Careers are now becoming jobs, because change is so rapid. Very few people can really develop a base from which to grow. In the quest for "upward" incomes and mobility more and more people do their jobs on the road. This lack of in-depth time with others causes our nation of followers to be superficial at best. Drugs seem to be more predictable than human relationships. Alcohol and pot are seen more and more as central focuses at parties, not the people and the conversation. Talk shows take care of our conversation need by replacing our discussion skills with those of a million dollar a year host.

Imagine leaders sold on the notion that they are in careers while the new workers feel they are in jobs. Problem solving would be difficult at best. A career is a life style whereas a job is primarily a place to earn money. Our culture more and more is turning out people who focus on how much they can make with job security rather than the focusing on what they can contribute. This new cultural norm with re-runs and multiple channel selections having few demands more than seven minutes long between the commercials, has produced a nation of young professionals who view time and goal oriented behavior differently.

Punctuality and work schedules tied to day and night cycles are of limited value in today's society where transactions are done by phone and mail. Time schedules might be intolerable to the current batch of students who feel time is more related to social rather than school needs. Flexible time is "in" and job controlled time is losing as a common value. We in education are just now realizing its effects on our planning for educational building and programming. Total days, each consisting of a.m., p.m., and night work is a reality when you have as many people employed as we in the U.S.A. now have.

The control of time allowed a degree of standardization of the flow of activities. Today there is a return to customize, not standardize. Educators went through that "individualization" before the culture was accepting customizing. Thus, at a time when school funds are low and we are restandardizing to save money, the culture is diversifying even more.

The forces will bring many changes to our culture:

- Communications will increasingly include electronics and visual displays. Broad-minded people will be trained in one or more specific skill areas. This indicates secondary and post secondary education will become important, but people other than certified teachers may be delivering information in time frames as short as mini workshops and as long as two or three year re-training programs.

- Singles and elders may not feel schools are worthy of financial support.

- Suburbia will slow down in many ways and cities will continue to deteriorate in terms of services, but will grow as leisure centers.

- Political powers and parties will be of minimal concern and special interest and customized special issue groups will rule. Leadership with these types of atypical concerns is almost impossible. Single or special issue groups, hard-nosed and negative with limited knowledge of system cause and effect, will fight less and less fairly and stress will be a by-product for public administrators. Therefore, the future administrative leader may have to be trained in forecasting and poll analysis as well as social psychology.

- There will be between 29 and 34 million students in schools this next decade. Private groups will vie for the funds to teach them. Secondary educational groups (high schools, intermediate educational districts and community colleges, and technology schools) will be in competition with private teaching groups.

- Unions will be in trouble, but minority members wanting to advance will play the union game, so look for powerful union pressures to keep social promotions alive in secondary schools.

- Productivity will be a major social force with more and more of our goods being produced and designed overseas. This means we must increase the intellectual behavior of our students, because 60 percent of the work force will be in information jobs which demand something other than an assembly line.

The leaders in education will be forced to be clear about who they are and what their populations want their school to be, while pushing for more universal needs of the larger culture.

7. Summary

IF WE WANT to improve educational leaders, we can change them by training, or by modifying their leadership situations. Common sense suggests that it is much easier to change various aspects of the leader's job than to change the person. When we talk about leadership forces, we are talking about: fairly deeply ingrained personality factors; habits and forces influencing interactions with those being led; and environmental and cultural forces. These can not be changed easily.

Leaders' performances depend not only on the broader culture and their own personalities and histories, but also on the organizational factors. In particular, leaders' control, power, and influence are the results of multiple forces. Appropriate awareness and self exploration can improve the organizational situation. Whether or not these factors improve performance depends on the match between the leader's power and the motivational patterns and the norms of the staff being led.

To plan for and carry out a group assessment of your staff's attitudes, needs, and norms requires that certain risks be taken. The best leaders in a negative normed district will be hindered. Do that which is real for you. Someone must take responsibility to ensure that each of the forces is assessed. That responsibility may be shared by many, or taken by only one, depending on individual style.

Changes within a person can be; changes within a school *must be* even if the status quo is adequate. Top leadership should devote time and effort to allowing administrators to experience techniques designed to teach them how to modify their environment and their own job to fit their style of leadership.

We hope the concepts and experiential portions presented are accepted in the manner in which we intended—as suggestive, not prescriptive.

Selected References

Bennis, Warren. *Organizational Development: Its Nature, Origins, and Prospects*. Reading, Mass: Addison-Wesley Co., Inc., 1969.

Blake, R. R. and Mouton, J. S. *The Managerial Grid*. Houston: Gulf Publishing Co., 1964.

Druker, Peter F. *Managing in Turbulent Times*. Philadelphia: Harper and Row, 1980.

Fielder, Fred. "Style or Circumstances: The Leadership Enigma," *Psychology Today*, March 1969.

Giammatteo, Michael C. *Rings Around Your Mind*. Vancouver, Wash.: Sylvan Institute, 1976.

Giammatteo, Michael C., and Dolores M. *Executive Well-Being*. Reston, Va.: NASSP, 1980.

Herzberg, Frederick, "Job Attitudes: Research and Opinion," Psychological Service of Pittsburgh, Pa., 1957.

_____"One More Time: How Do You Motivate Employees?" *Harvard Business Review*, Jan.–Feb., 1968.

Maslow, Abraham H. *Motivation and Personality*. New York: Harper and Row, 1954.

McGregor, Douglas M. "The Human Side of Enterprise," *Management Review*, Nov. 1957.

Myers, M. Scott, "Who Are Your Motivated Workers?" *Harvard Business Review*, XLII, Jan.–Feb., 1964.

Russell, G. H., and Black, Kenneth, Jr. *Human Behavior in Business*. New Jersey: Prentice-Hall, 1972.